THE MUSICALS SONGBOOK

MICHAEL BURNETT

MUSIC DEPARTMENT
OXFORD UNIVERSITY PRESS
OXFORD AND NEW YORK

Oxford University Press, Walton Street, Oxford OX2 6DP, England

Oxford is a trade mark of Oxford University Press
© Oxford University Press 1990

No part of this publication may be reproduced, stored in a retrieval system, or transmitted, in any form or by any means, electronic, mechanical, photocopying, recording, or otherwise, without the prior permission of the Publishers

This book is sold subject to the condition that it shall not, by way of trade or otherwise, be lent, re-sold, hired out or otherwise circulated without the publisher's prior consent in any form of binding or cover other than that in which it is published and without a similar condition including this condition being imposed on the subsequent purchaser

Acknowledgements

'The Deadwood Stage' from *Calamity Jane*, words and music by Sammy Fain/Paul Francis Webster © Remick Music Corp. Reproduced by kind permission of Warner Bros Music Ltd. 'Consider Yourself', 'I'd Do Anything' by Lionel Bart © 1959 Lakeview Music Publishing Co. Ltd., 7 Bury Place, London WC7A 2LA, for the world excluding W. Hemisphere, (USA, Central and South America, Mexico, Cuba, Canada, Australasia, and South Africa) International copyright secured. All rights reserved. Used by permission. 'Over the Rainbow' words by E. Y. Harburg, Music by Harold Arlen © 1938, 1939 (Renewed 1966, 1967) Metro-Goldwyn-Mayer Inc. All rights controlled and administered by Leo Feist Inc., a catalog of CBS songs, a division of CBS Inc. International copyright secured. All rights reserved. Used by permission. 'We're Off to see the Wizard' words by E. Y. Harburg, music by Harold Arlen. © 1939 (Renewed 1967) Metro-Goldwyn-Mayer Inc. All rights controlled and administered by Leo Feist Inc., a catalog of CBS songs, a division of CBS Inc. International copyright secured. All rights reserved. Used by permisison. 'Do-re-mi', 'Oh what a beautiful mornin'', 'My favourite things' and 'I whistle a happy tune' by Rodgers and Hammerstein; 'Flash bang wallop!' by Heneker; 'The White Horse Inn' by Benatzky and Graham; 'I got plenty o' nuttin'' by Gershwin and Heyward; 'Maria' by Bernstein and Sondheim. Reproduced by kind permission of Chappell Music Ltd.

Many thanks to Michael Stimpson for his work on the guitar chords.

Music Department
OXFORD UNIVERSITY PRESS
Oxford

CONTENTS

1. **Do-re-mi** *The Sound of Music*
2. **Flash, bang, wallop!** *Half a Sixpence*
3. **The White Horse Inn** *The White Horse Inn*
4. **I got plenty o' nuttin'** *Porgy and Bess*
5. **Oh what a beautiful mornin'** *Oklahoma!*
6. **Consider yourself at home** *Oliver!*
7. **Over the rainbow** *The Wizard of Oz*
8. **My favourite things** *The Sound of Music*
9. **The Deadwood stage** *Calamity Jane*
10. **Maria** *West Side Story*
11. **I whistle a happy tune** *The King and I*
12. **We're off to see the Wizard** *The Wizard of Oz*

This book contains a varied selection of songs from some of the most popular musicals. Every song is provided with a piano accompaniment and optional chord symbols for guitar or electronic keyboard. A second optional accompaniment is also included, this being suitable for a wide range of instruments including descant recorder, violin, flute, and electronic keyboard. Background information, both on the songs and on the musicals from which they have been taken, is also provided.

The Musicals Songbook contains a song for everyone, and music teachers in upper primary, middle and secondary schools, and also youth clubs, will find the collection of particular relevance to their needs.

Michael Burnett

The Sound of Music

do re mi

'Do-re-mi' is just one of the many popular tunes which resulted from the collaboration of Richard Rodgers and Oscar Hammerstein II. It is taken from their last musical, *The Sound of Music*, which was first produced in 1959 and went on to become a huge box office success on Broadway. Another song from *The Sound of Music*, 'My favourite things', can be found on page 39.

The story is set in Austria at the end of the 1930s and was inspired by a book, *The Trapp Family Singers*, which described the musical activities of a real family. Maria is training to be a nun at Nonnberg Abbey but is not considered dedicated enough for religious life. She is, therefore, sent away to become the governess to the seven children of Captain von Trapp, a widower. The children grow fond of Maria, who is an imaginative teacher who shares with them her love of music and singing ('Do-re-mi'). However, when the Captain brings Elsa, his fiancée, to the house, Maria realizes that she is herself in love with him, and consequently returns to the Abbey. Here, the Abbess shows great sympathy and advises her to 'Climb every mountain' in the attempt to gain true happiness; so Maria goes back to the Trapp house, only to discover that the Captain has broken off the engagement as a result of Elsa's pro-Nazi views. Eventually he marries Maria instead, at a ceremony in the Abbey; however, the Nazi take-over of Austria puts the Captain in danger, and the entire family is forced to flee over the mountains to freedom.

1
Do-re-mi
Oscar Hammerstein and Richard Rodgers

© Oxford University Press 1990

OXFORD UNIVERSITY PRESS, MUSIC DEPARTMENT, WALTON STREET, OXFORD OX2 6DP
Photocopying this copyright material is ILLEGAL.

Printed in Great Britain

Half a Sixpence

Flash, bang, wallop!

This song is from *Half a sixpence*, which was first performed at the Cambridge Theatre in London during 1963, with Tommy Steele playing the lead part. The musical is based on H. G. Wells' novel *Kipps*, which had previously been made both into a play and a film.

David Heneker's version introduces us to the orphan, Kipps, as a young man. Kipps works as an apprentice shopman and is in love with Ann, whom he has known since childhood. The two seal their love by each keeping a half of a sixpenny piece specially cut in two. However, as Kipps becomes richer and more successful, he begins to mix with high society and is attracted to an upper-class girl, Helen. Eventually he realises that it is still Ann whom he loves and wishes to marry, and the two, together with their half-sixpences, are reunited. 'Flash, bang, wallop!' is sung by Kipps and the supporting cast after the wedding has taken place.

2
Flash, bang, wallop!
David Heneker

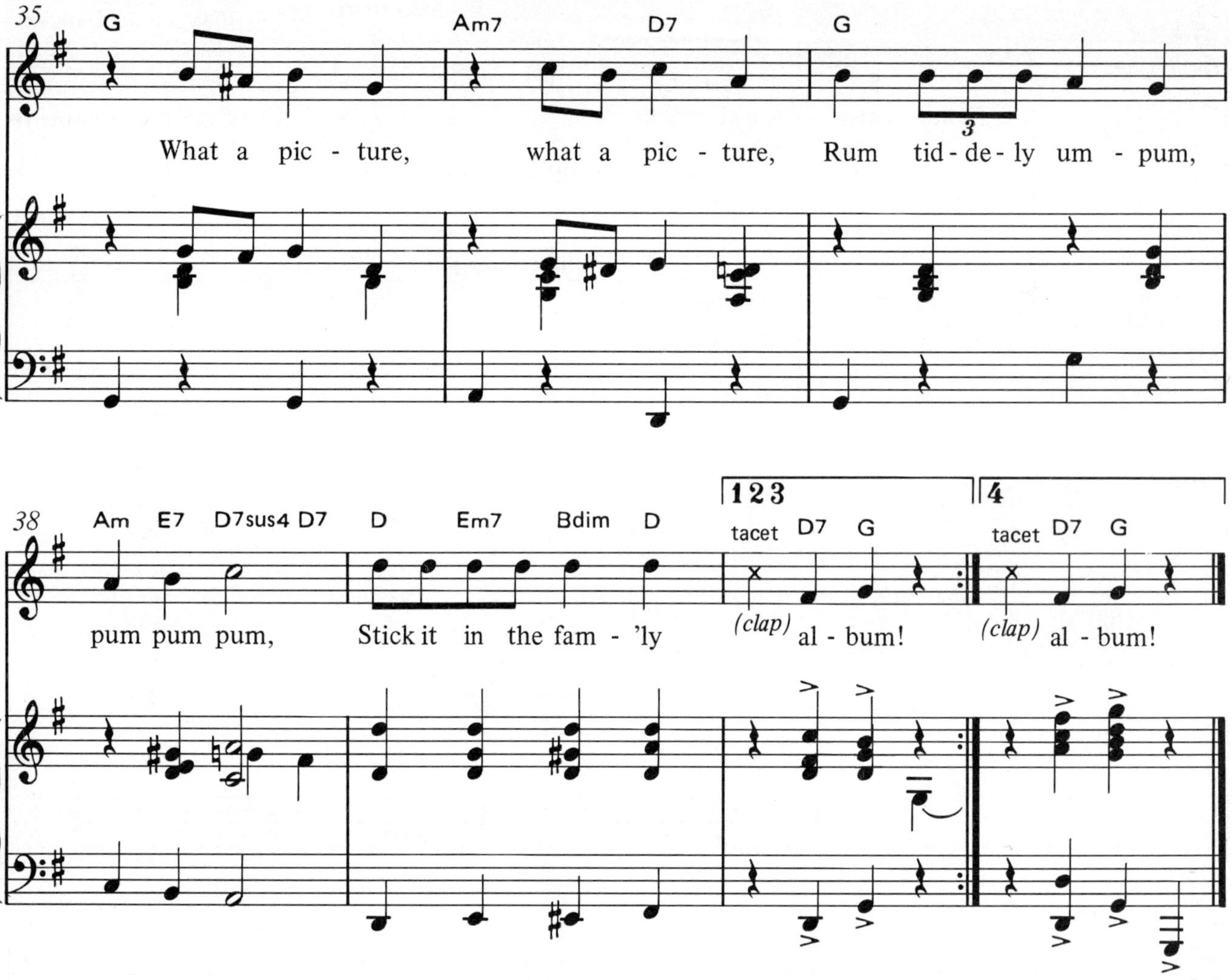
35
G Am7 D7 G
What a pic - ture, what a pic - ture, Rum tid - de - ly um - pum,
3
38
Am E7 D7sus4 D7 D Em7 Bdim D
pum pum pum, Stick it in the fam - 'ly
1 2 3
tacet D7 G
(clap) al - bum!
4
tacet D7 G
(clap) al - bum!

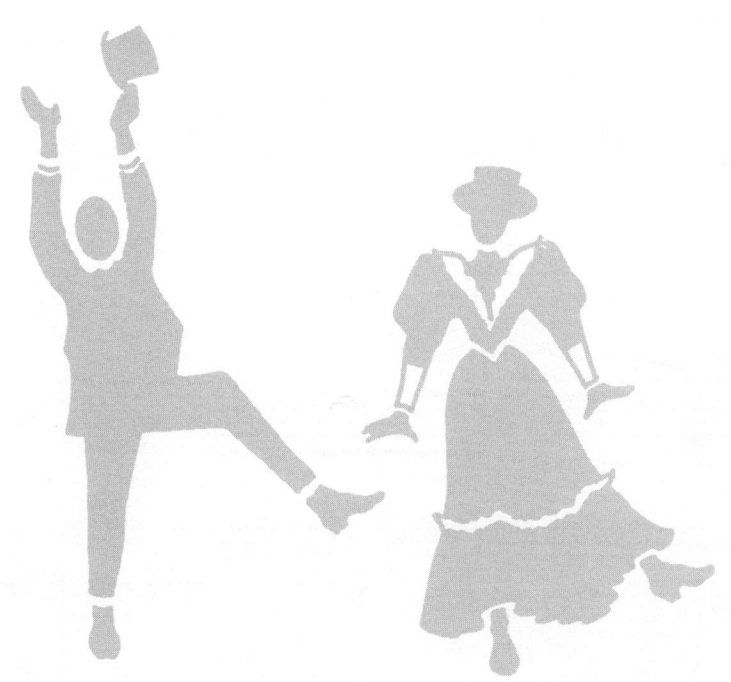

The White Horse Inn

White Horse Inn

The White Horse Inn is the best-known song from the musical of the same name, a light-hearted love-story set in Austria before the First World War. It is the height of the season in the busy tourist resort of St Wolfgang, and the popular White Horse Inn has a constant stream of guests. Among these is a regular visitor, Dr Siedler, to whom Josefa, the landlady of the Inn, has taken a fancy. However, Leopold, the headwaiter, is himself in love with Josefa and suffers great pangs of jealousy. In fact, he becomes so beside himself that he bursts into tears instead of making his speech of welcome when the Emperor Franz Josef arrives with the intention of staying at The White Horse Inn.

All ends well, though, when the Emperor tells Josefa that she would never be happy living in the city with Dr Siedler. Instead, she agrees to marry Leopold and remain with him at the Inn, where, in the words of the song, 'There's sunshine ever in store'.

The White Horse Inn was first staged in Berlin in 1930, and was put on at the London Coliseum the following year.

3
The White Horse Inn
Robert Gilbert and Ralph Benatzky

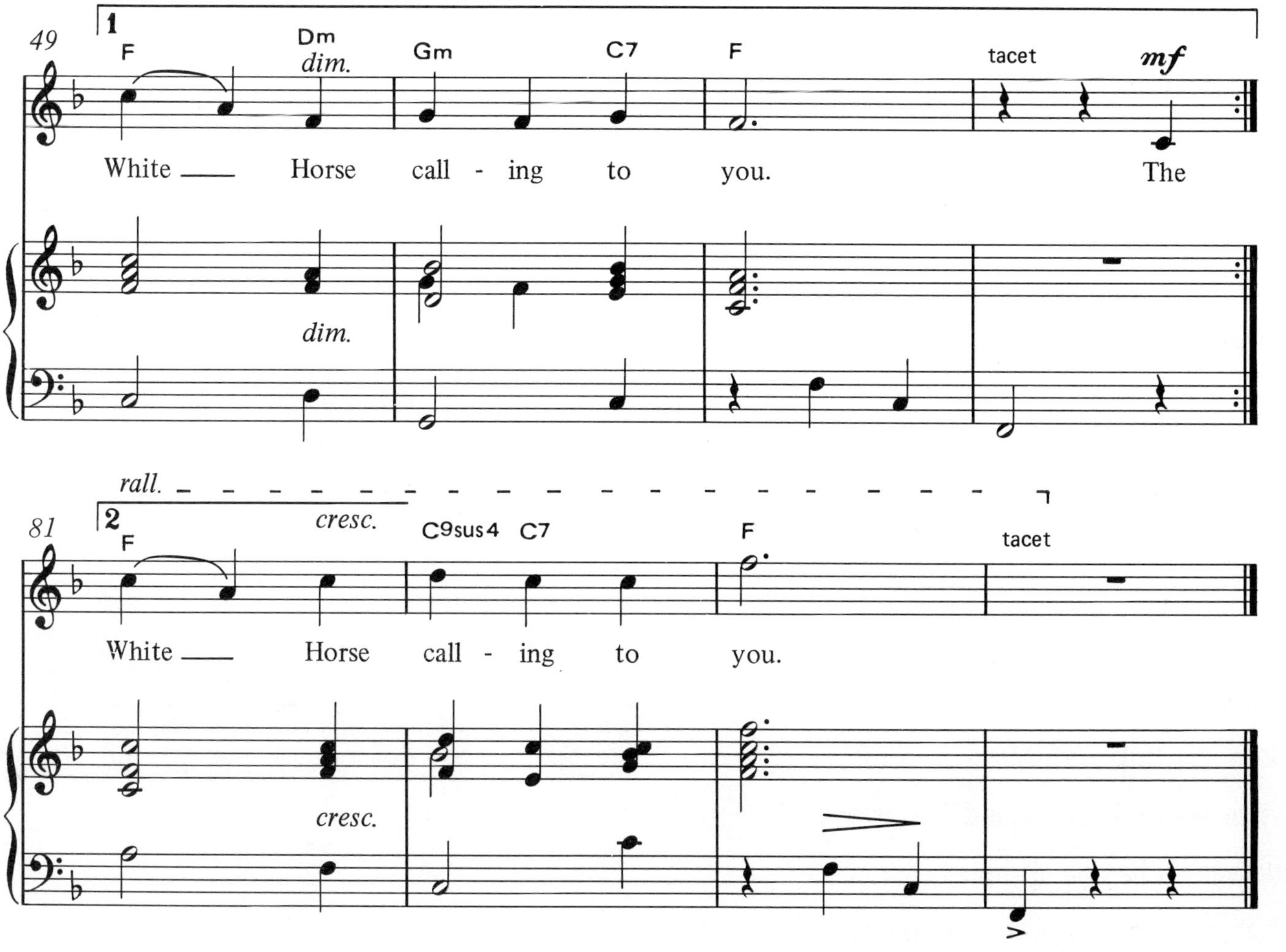
49
1
F Dm Gm C7 F tacet
dim.
mf
White — Horse call - ing to you. The
dim.
rall.
81
2
F C9sus4 C7 F tacet
cresc.
White — Horse call - ing to you.
cresc.

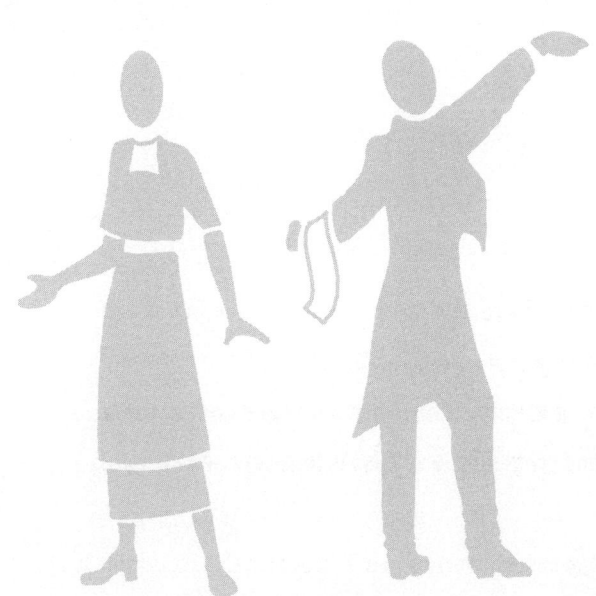

Porgy and Bess

I got plenty o' nuttin'

This song comes from the opera *Porgy and Bess*, by George Gershwin. Gershwin was an American classical composer who looked to jazz for inspiration, and the opera, like his *Rhapsody in blue* for piano and orchestra, has many rhythmic, melodic, and harmonic ideas which are derived from this black American form. *Porgy and Bess* was first performed in 1935, when one critic described it as 'a joy to hear'. It has an all-black cast of characters and is set in Charleston, a seaport in South Carolina.

The story is complicated and sometimes violent. Its main characters live in Catfish Row, a run-down part of the town, and the plot centres on the relationship between Bess and the two men in her life, Crown and Porgy. Crown has a free and easy attitude to life while Porgy, a cripple, is kind and protective, and Bess is torn between the two. In the end Crown is killed by Porgy.

In 'I got plenty o' nuttin'', Porgy sings of his poverty and will to survive. In its original version the song has a strummed, oom-pah, banjo accompaniment. Other well-known tunes from *Porgy and Bess* include 'Summertime' and 'A woman is a sometime thing'.

4
I got plenty o' nuttin'
George Gershwin

Oklahoma!

Oh what a beautiful mornin'

This song is taken from *Oklahoma!*, a musical which broke all existing records for box office receipts and length of run when it was first staged on Broadway in 1943. Many critics had predicted a flop for Rodgers and Hammerstein, saying that the musical lacked star roles, humour, and the dance routines needed for success. Certainly *Oklahoma!* did not conform to the traditional mould in terms of style and content; but its serious plot and use of ideas from American folk ballet struck a chord of relevance to audiences of the time.

The setting is the State of Oklahoma early this century, and the musical opens to the sound of Curly singing 'Oh what a beautiful mornin'' as he makes his way to Aunt Eller's farmhouse to invite her niece, Laurey, to a box-social that evening. (A box-social is a dance at which the girls auction food boxes, the men bidding for the boxes of the girls of their choice.) Laurey, although in love with Curly, decides to go to the social with Jud, an employee on the farm, hoping to make Curly jealous in the process. However, Jud is disappointed when she decides to accompany Curly after all, and the seeds of disaster are sown.

At the social Curly buys Laurey's box at an exorbitant price, and the two decide to marry. The ceremony takes place three weeks later and Jud, drunk, barges in during the celebrations, threatening Curly with a knife. A brawl takes place during which Jud falls on the knife and is killed. Curly is accused of having caused the death, and a trial is held, but he is acquitted and the couple are allowed to proceed with their honeymoon.

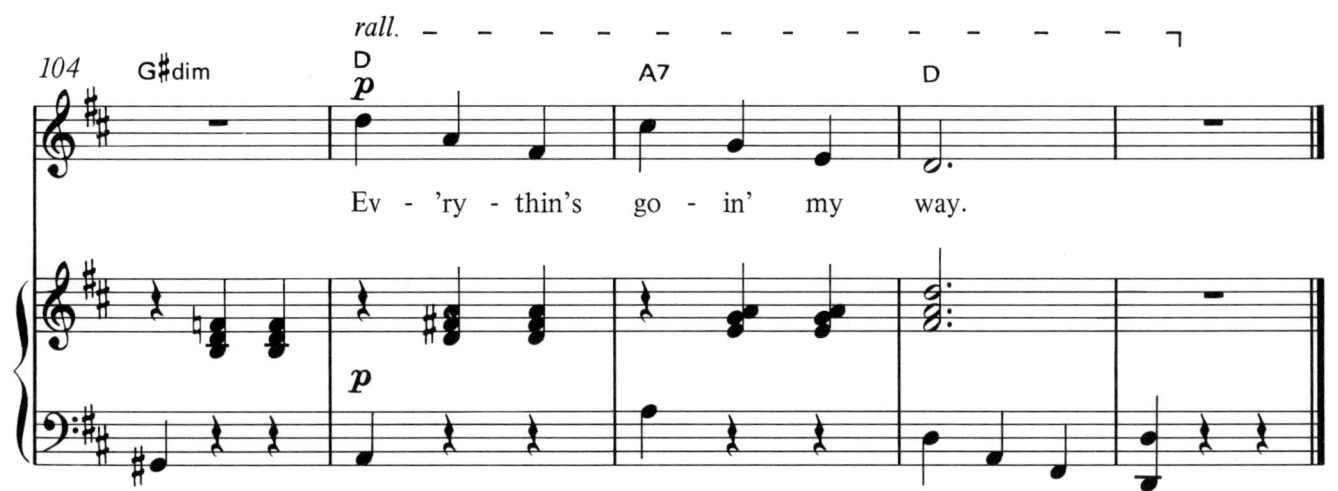

Oliver!

Consider yourself at home

Lionel Bart's adaptation of Charles Dickens' popular novel *Oliver Twist* was first performed in London in 1960. The story has some scenes which lend themselves well to staging and music, and the composer makes the most of these—for example, the well-known workhouse scene with which the musical begins. Here, the boys of the workhouse, hungry and faced with their usual meal of one ladleful of thin gruel, sing of all the 'Food, glorious food' which they would so much rather have to eat: 'hot sausage and mustard', for example, and 'peaches and cream about six feet high'.

The climax of the scene occurs when Oliver plucks up enough courage to speak out. 'Please sir', he says to Mr Bumble, the man in charge of the workhouse, 'I want some more!' Mr Bumble is furious, of course, and turns Oliver out of the workhouse, with the result that Oliver meets the Artful Dodger and becomes a member of Fagin's band of thieves. 'Consider yourself at home' is first sung by the Dodger as he welcomes Oliver to a life of crime.

Lionel Bart's musical contains several other well-known songs including 'Where is love?', 'Pick a pocket or two' and 'I'd do anything'.

6
Consider yourself at home
Lionel Bart

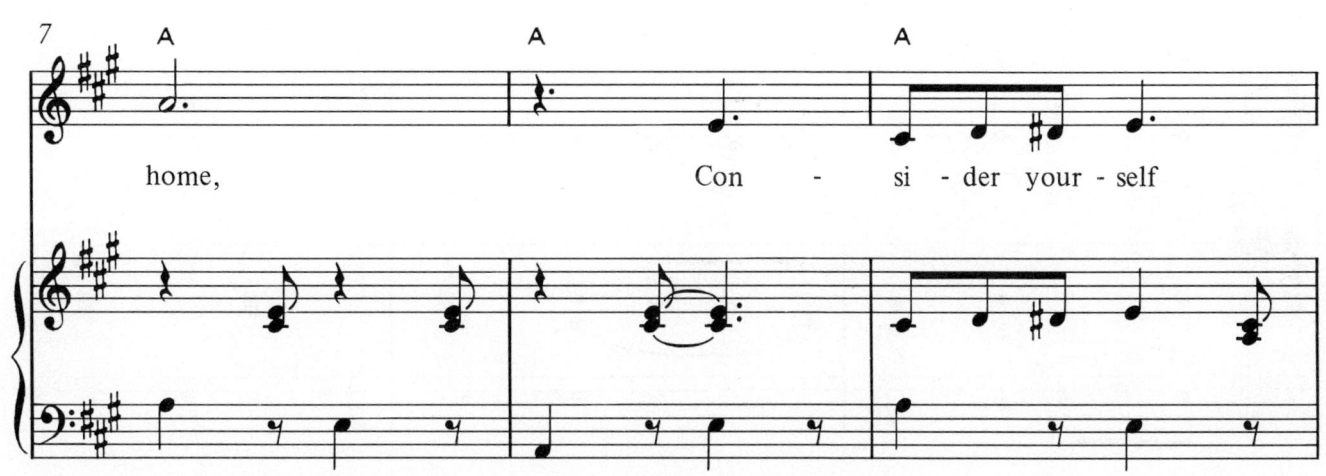

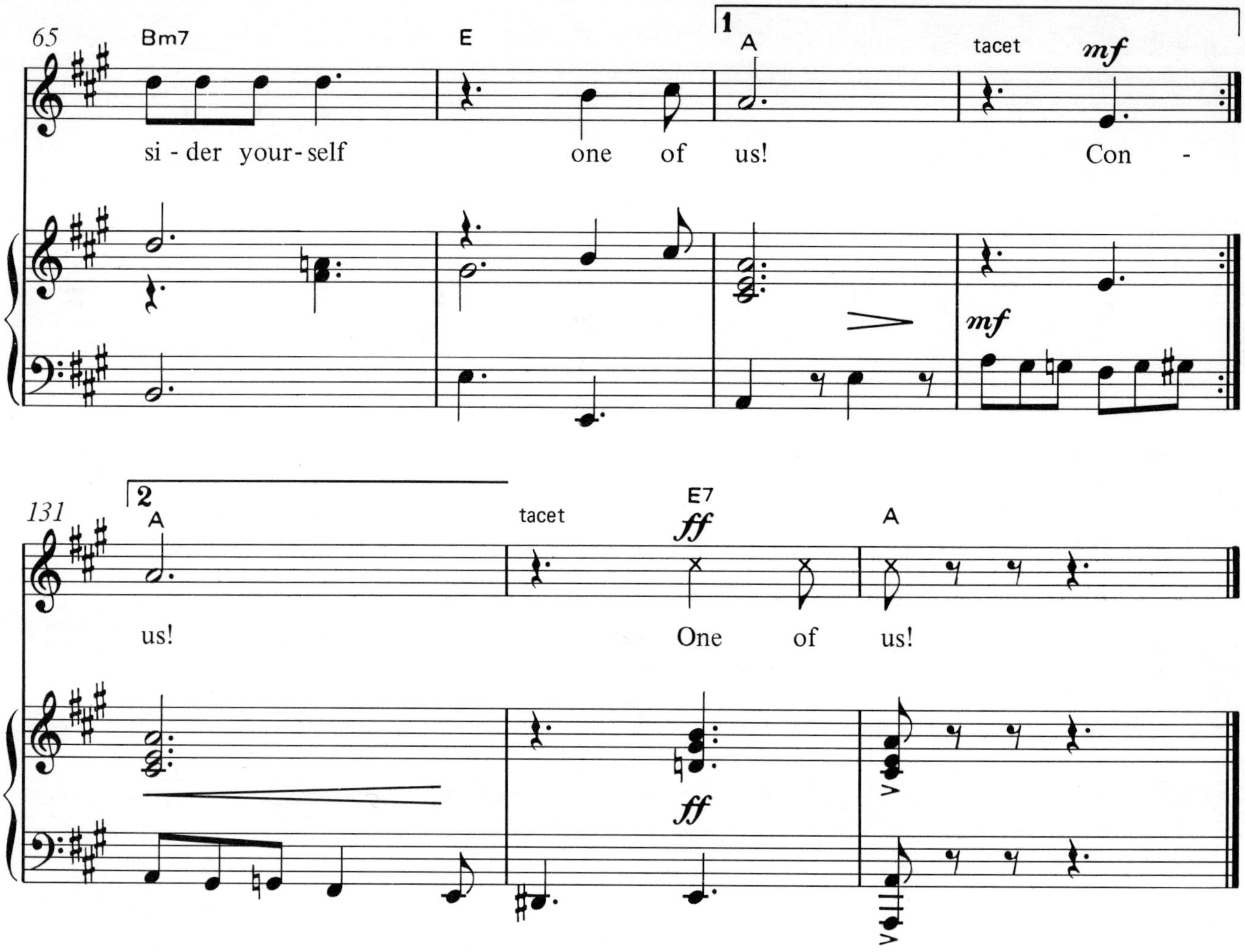
65
Bm7
E
1
A
tacet
mf
si - der your - self
one of us!
Con -
mf
131
2
A
tacet
E7
ff
A
us!
One of us!
ff

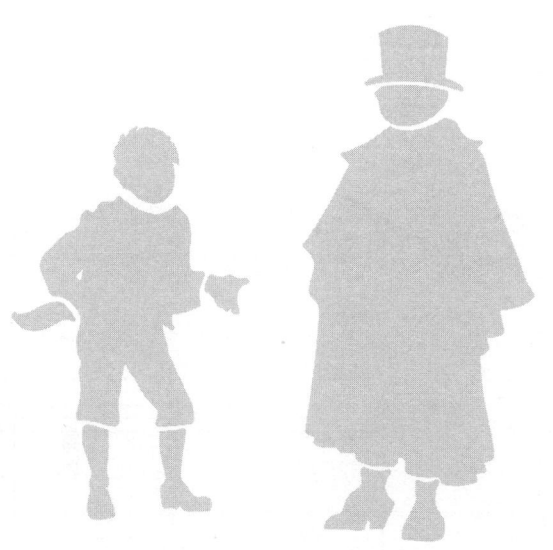

The Wizard of Oz

People have been captivated by the story of *The Wizard of Oz* for more than 80 years. It first appeared as a novel by Frank Baum, who then adapted the story so that it could be made into a musical, which was staged in 1903 at New York's Majestic Theatre. Much later, in 1939, the musical was turned into a film, which starred Judy Garland as Dorothy. It was this version of *The Wizard of Oz* which became most famous, not only because of Judy Garland's brilliant performance, but also because of the completely new music which had been written by Harold Arlen to E. Y. Harburg's new lyrics. 'Over the rainbow' won an Academy Award and 'We're off to see the Wizard' (page 60) became one of the best-known of all tunes from musicals.

The Wizard of Oz is a modern fairy tale which offers producers many opportunities for special effects. It also has the quality of a dream, for which Dorothy's song 'Over the rainbow' sets the scene. A hurricane carries Dorothy, together with the Kansas farmhouse in which she lives, up and away to the land of Oz. There Dorothy meets Scarecrow, who has lost his brain, Tinman, who has no heart, and, later, a cowardly Lion. The four set off to find the Wizard of Oz in the hope that he will restore the missing brain, heart, and courage, and Dorothy to Kansas. After a number of adventures, they do in fact, meet up with him and all ends happily when he grants their requests.

over the rainbow

7
Over the rainbow
E. Y. Harburg and Harold Arlen

Moderato

Guitar tacet

When all the world is a hope-less jum-ble and the rain-drops tum-ble all a-round, Hea-ven o-pens a ma-gic

11
D tacet D G
lane. When all the clouds dar-ken up the sky-way There's a
15
Dmaj7 C♯m7 F♯7 Bm G9 Esus4 E7
rain - bow high-way to be found, lead - ing from your win - dow
19
A G D Bdim Em A7
pane to a place be-hind the sun,
22
D Bdim Em A7sus4 A7
just a step be-yond the rain.

Some-where o-ver the rain-bow way up high,

There's a land that I heard of once in a lul-la-by.

Some-where o-ver the rain-bow skies are blue,

And the dreams that you dare to dream real-ly do come true.

true. Some day I'll wish up-on a star and wake up when the clouds are far be-hind me, _____ Where trou-bles melt like le-mon drops, a-way, a-bove the chim-ney tops, that's where you'll find me.

a tempo

Some - where o - ver the rain - bow blue - birds

fly, Birds fly o-ver the rain-bow, why then, oh why can't I? If hap-py lit-tle blue-birds fly be-yond the rain-bow, why oh why can't I?

The Sound of Music

My favourite things

'My favourite things' is another song from Rodger and Hammerstein's highly successful *The Sound of Music* (see page 2 for 'Do-re-mi', also from the musical and page 1 for a fuller description of the plot).

The first scene of *The Sound of Music* is set in Nonnberg Abbey, Austria, where it is becoming apparent that the novice, Maria, is not single-minded enough to dedicate her life to religion alone. For example, she would rather spend time on a mountain-top singing of the joys of nature ('The sound of music') than doing the duties of a nun.

In the light of this, the Abbess decides that Maria should be sent away in order to become a governess. But not before the Abbess herself admits to sharing, with Maria, those pleasures of life which she describes in 'My favourite things' . . .

8
My favourite things
Oscar Hammerstein and Richard Rodgers

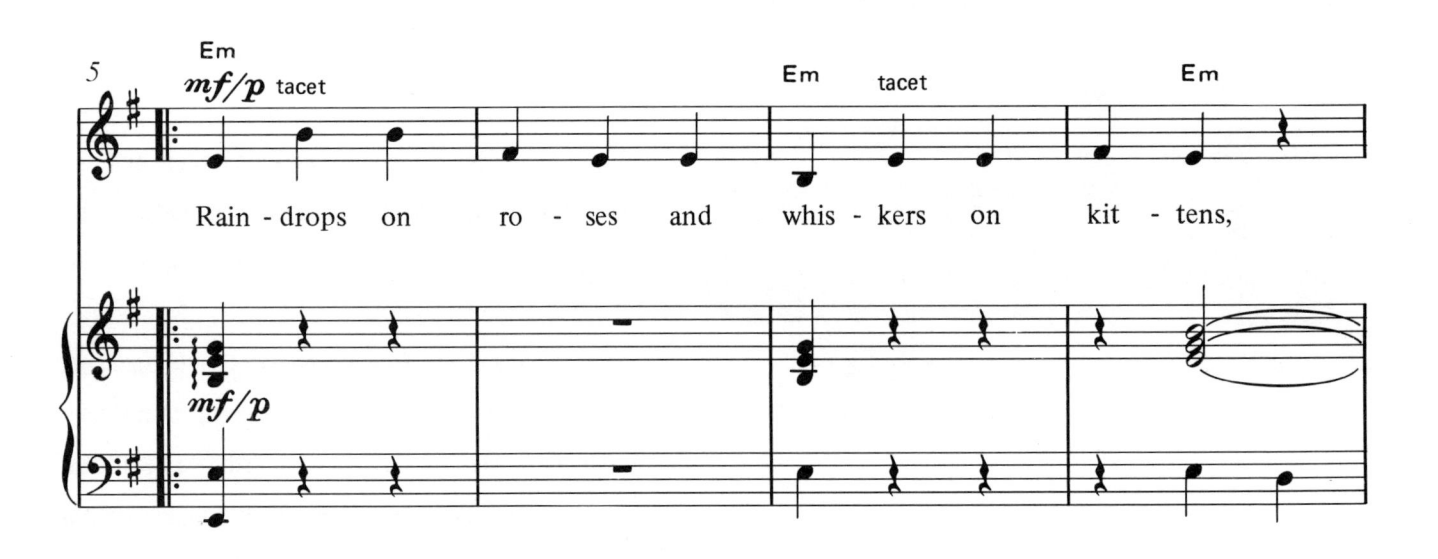

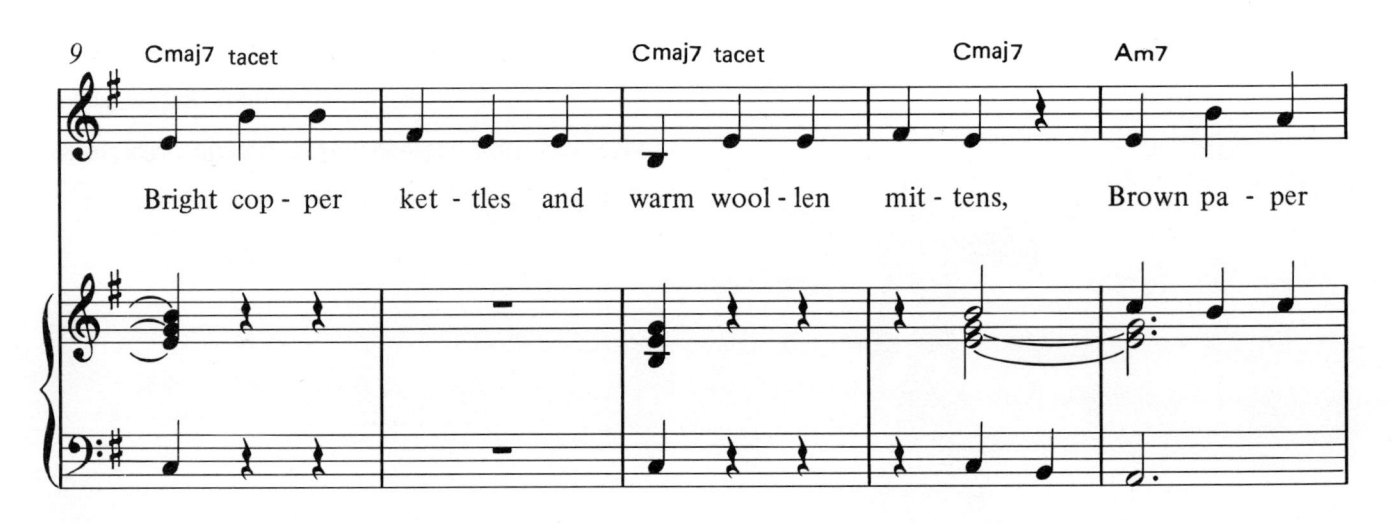

Con moto

Guitar tacet

Rain-drops on ro-ses and whis-kers on kit-tens,

Bright cop-per ket-tles and warm wool-len mit-tens, Brown pa-per

14
D
Bm7
C
G
C
pack - ag - es tied up with strings, These are a few of my
19
Am♯6
B
B
B7
Em
f/mp
fa - vour - ite things. Cream co - loured
f/mp
24
Em
Em
Em
Cmaj7
pon - ies and crisp ap - ple stru - dels, Door - bells and
28
Cmaj7
Cmaj7
Cmaj7
Am7
sleigh - bells and schnit - zel with noo - dles, Wild geese that

fly with the moon on their wings, These are a few of my fa-vour-ite things

Girls in white dress-es with blue sa-tin sash-es, Snow-flakes that stay on my nose and eye-lash-es, Sil-ver white

winters that melt in-to springs These are a few of my fa-vour-ite things. When the dog bites, When the bee stings, When I'm feel-ing sad, I simp-ly re-mem-ber my fa - vour - ite things and then I don't feel so bad!

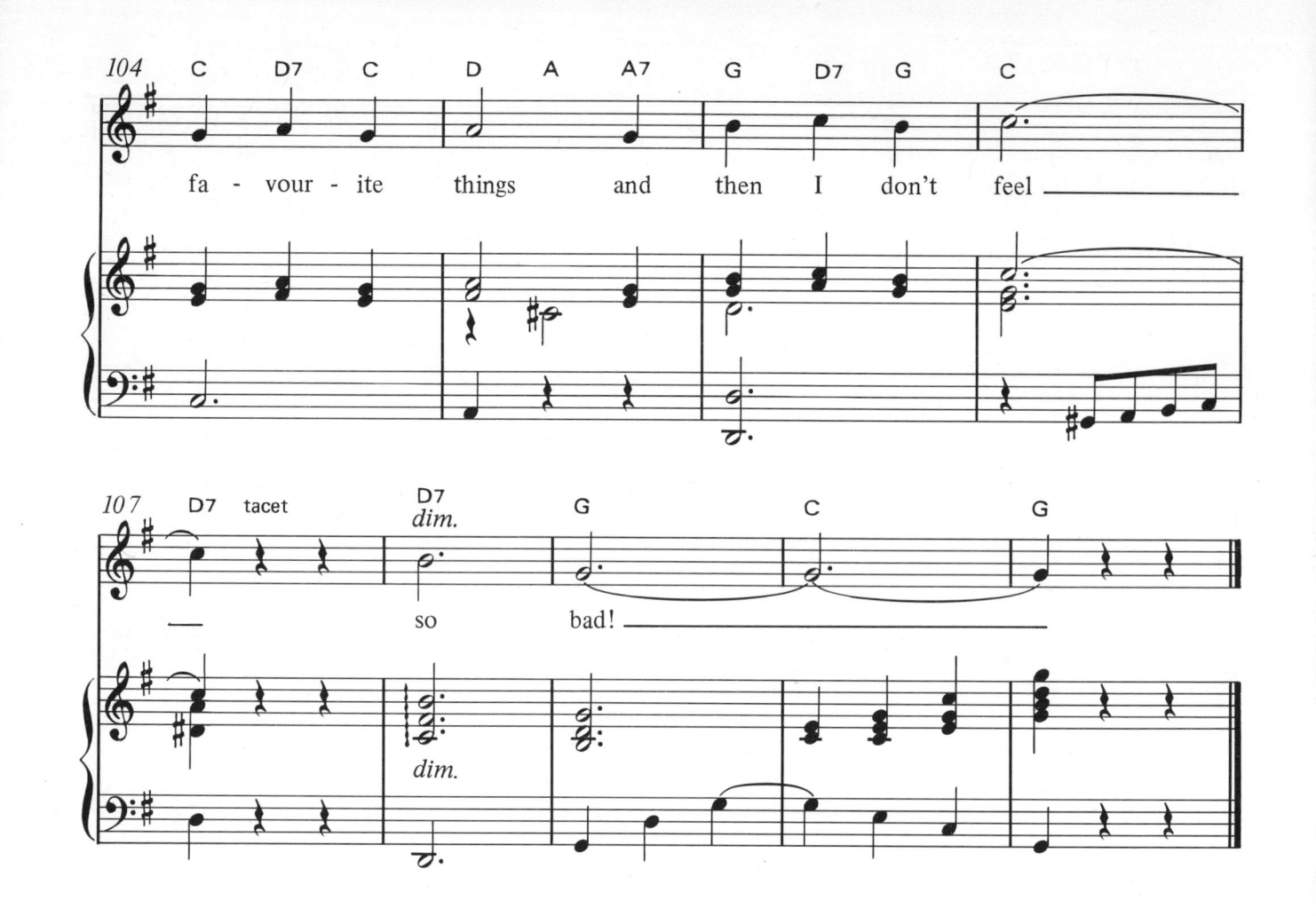

Calamity Jane

The Deadwood Stage

The year is 1876, the setting America's Wild West, and over the Black Hills of Dakota Territory comes a stagecoach bound for Deadwood City. The coach is loaded with passengers and all kinds of goods —'snake oil fer rheumatism', 'a genuine string of artificial pearls'— and is escorted, on horseback, by a 'hard-bitten, gun-totin'' woman.

'The Deadwood Stage' is the opening number of Webster and Fain's famous musical *Calamity Jane*, in which we learn that Calamity is not so 'hard-bitten' after all. For, despite her bravado and apparent toughness, she falls in love with a young army officer, Lieutenant Danny Martin. However, Danny loves Katie, a stage-struck young lady from Chicago who is in no doubt concerning her feelings towards him: 'Love you dearly, words can't express it clearly, You seem to take my very breath away'. A further complication is that Calamity is, in turn, loved by Wild Bill Hickock, a professional gambler who spends much of his time at the bar of The Golden Garter, 'where the cream of Deadwood City comes to dine'. Eventually true love has its way, and Calamity realises that she has secretly been in love with Wild Bill all along. The realisation sets the scene for the musical's grand finale, the double wedding of Danny and Katie, Calamity and Bill.

9
The Deadwood stage
Paul Webster and Sammy Fain

Rhythmically
Guitar tacet

1. Oh, the Dead-wood Stage is a roll-in' on ov-er the plains _____ with the cur-tains flap-pin' an' the
   Dead-wood Stage is a head-in' on ov-er the hills _____ where the In-jun ar-rows are a

46

dri - ver a - slap-pin' the reins.
thick - er than por - ker - pine quills.

Beau - ti - ful sky   A won - der - ful day.
Dan - ger - ous land   No time to de - lay.

Whip crack a - way, whip crack a - way, whip crack a -

way.   2. Oh, the way.

47

3. They're head-in' straight for town loaded down with a fancy car-go care of Wells and Far-go, Il-li-nois. _____ Boy! Oh, the Dead-wood Stage is a-com-in' on ov-er the crest _____ like a

4. The wheels go turn-in' round, home-ward bound, can't cha hear 'em hum-min'? Hap-py times a-com-in' fer to stay. _____ Hey! They'll be home to-night by the light of the sil-ver-y moon, _____ an' their

hom - in' pig - eon that's a - han - ker - in' af - ter its nest.
hearts a - thump - in' like a man - do - lin plunk - in' a tune!

Twen - ty - three miles they've
When they get home they'll be

cov - ered to - day.
fix - in' to stay.

Whip crack a - way, whip crack a - way, whip crack a - way. way. Hey!

West Side Story

MARIA

Leonard Bernstein was already one of America's most important classical composers when he decided to turn his hand to writing a musical. *West Side Story*, with its famous love-song 'Maria', was the result, and it could hardly have been a greater success. Indeed, *West Side Story* was described as a 'sensational hit' after its first performance in 1957, both because of its catchy tunes and rhythms, and its up-to-date story set in the slums of New York.

Here, two teenage gangs, the Jets and the Sharks, are at each other's throats; yet Tony, one of the Jets, has fallen in love with Maria, whose brother belongs to the Sharks. The love is mutual, and the two have a secret affair which is doomed from the start. The gang warfare continues, and Tony is provoked into killing Maria's brother after the latter has stabbed one of the Jets. Maria forgives Tony, but he is, in the end, shot by a member of the Sharks.

West Side Story is well-known for its dramatic dance-scenes, in which the gang warfare is portrayed. 'Tonight' is another popular song from the musical.

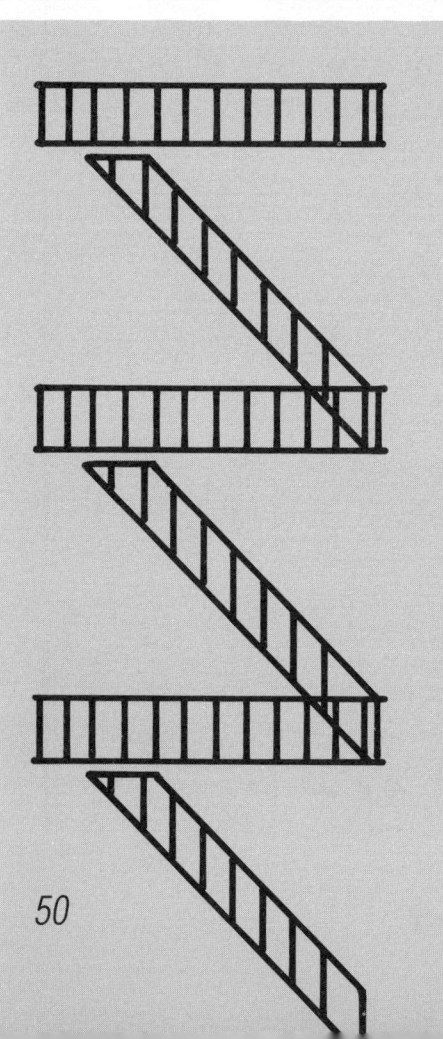

10
Maria
Stephen Sondheim and Leonard Bernstein

Ma- ri - a! ___ I've just met a girl named Ma - ri - a, ___ And sud-den-ly that name Will ne-ver be the same To me. Ma-ri - a! — I've just met a girl named Ma - ri - a, — And sud-den-ly I've found How won-der-ful a sound Can be! Ma - ri - a! Say it loud and there's mu - sic play-ing, Say it soft and it's al - most like pray-ing. Ma - ri - a, — I'll

23 Gm/A　　　　　　　　　D　　　　　　tacet

ne - ver stop say - ing Ma - ri - a.＿＿ Ma - ri - a!＿＿ Ma-

46　　　rall.　　　　　　　　　　　Dmaj7
　　　　mp

ri - a!＿＿ I've just met a girl named Ma - ri - a.＿＿

The King and I

I whistle a happy tune

During the 1860s Anna Leonowens, accompanied by her son Louis, arrives at the Palace of the King of Siam to take up the position of governess to his children. She sings 'I whistle a happy tune' to keep up her spirits in a new, daunting situation.

This is the opening scene of Rodgers and Hammerstein's *The King and I*, first staged in 1951 with Yul Brynner playing the King. Other well-known songs from the musical include 'Hello, young lovers' and 'Shall we dance?' The plot is a complex one which centres on the development of the relationship between Anna, an educated western woman, and the King, the autocratic ruler of an eastern state.

The climax of the musical is a ball, thrown by the King with Anna's help, in honour of visiting English dignitaries. The success of the ball is marred, however, by the discovery that Tuptim, a Burmese slave, has attempted to escape from the Palace with her lover Lun Tha, the latter having been killed in the process. Not for the first time, Anna intercedes on behalf of Tuptim and prevails upon the King to withdraw his order that she should be whipped. Later, the King becomes ill and, on his death-bed, asks Anna to remain in Siam to look after his children. She agrees to this request, much to the delight of the children, who have grown to love their governess.

11
I whistle a happy tune
Oscar Hammerstein and Richard Rodgers

Rhythmically

Whenever I feel afraid I hold my head erect And whistle a happy
Shivering in my shoes I strike a careless pose And whistle a happy

tune So no one will sus-pect I'm a-
tune And no one ev - er

fraid. While knows I'm a-fraid.

The re-sult of this de - cep - tion is

ve - ry strange to tell For when I fool the

people I fear I fool myself as well! I whistle a happy tune And ev-'ry single time The happiness in the tune con-vinces me that I'm not afraid.

Make be-lieve you're brave And the trick will take you far. You may be as brave As you make be-lieve you are.

(whistle)

You may be as brave As you make be-lieve you are. When

The Wizard of Oz

WE'RE OFF TO SEE THE WIZARD

This is another song from the 1939 film version of Frank Baum's famous *The Wizard of Oz* (see page 34 for 'Over the rainbow', also from the musical, and page 33 for a fuller description of the plot). It was this version which featured Judy Garland as Dorothy, the Kansas girl carried away by a hurricane to Oz, a magical land inhabited by the Munchkins.

Dorothy has many adventures during her journey, accompanied by Scarecrow, Tinman, and Lion, to find the Wizard, a 'Whiz of a Wiz if ever a Wiz there was' and capable of all manner of wonderful deeds. 'We're off to see the Wizard' is sung by Dorothy, Scarecrow, and Tinman at the beginning of their journey along the yellow brick road.

12
We're off to see the Wizard
E. Y. Harburg and Harold Arlen

Moderato
Guitar tacet

Fol-low the yel-low brick road, Fol-low the yel-low brick road, Fol-low, fol-low fol-low, fol-low, fol-low the yel-low brick

12
G C G9sus4 C
mp
road. Fol - low the yel - low brick road,
mp
15
C G9sus4 C C Dm7
Fol - low the yel - low brick road, Fol - low, fol - low,
18
F G7 Am D7 G
fol - low, fol - low, fol - low the yel - low brick road.
21
Dm7 G7 C Dm7 G7
mf
Fol - low the rain - bow ov - er the stream, Fol - low the fel - low who
mf

24
C
C Dm7
F G7
fol - lows a dream, Fol - low, fol - low, fol - low, fol - low,
27
Am7 D7
Am7 G7 cresc. G7
Fol - low the yel - low brick road. We're off, we're
cresc.
30
G7
G7
tacet G7
f
C Dm7
off, We're off. We're off to see the
f
34
C
Dm7 G7
C
Wiz - ard, the won - der - ful Wiz - ard of Oz. We

Lyrics:

hear he is a Whiz of a Wiz if ever a Wiz there was. If ever, oh ever, a Wiz there was, The Wizard of Oz is one becoz, be-coz, be-coz, be-coz, be-coz, be-coz, Be-coz of the wonderful things he does.

(whistle) We're off to see the Wiz-ard, The won-der-ful Wiz-ard of Oz. Oz.

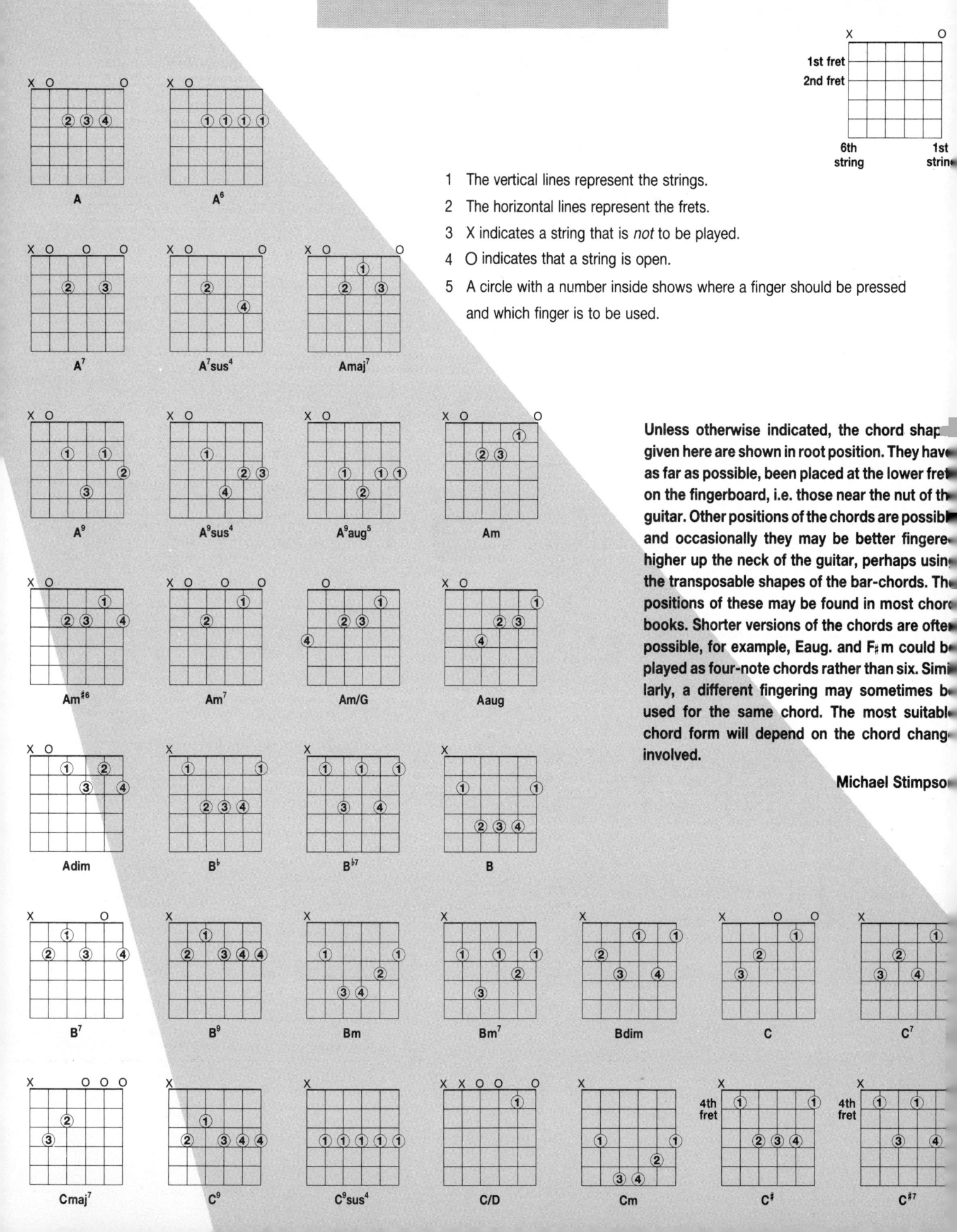

GUITAR CHORDS

1. The vertical lines represent the strings.
2. The horizontal lines represent the frets.
3. X indicates a string that is *not* to be played.
4. O indicates that a string is open.
5. A circle with a number inside shows where a finger should be pressed and which finger is to be used.

Unless otherwise indicated, the chord shapes given here are shown in root position. They have, as far as possible, been placed at the lower frets on the fingerboard, i.e. those near the nut of the guitar. Other positions of the chords are possible and occasionally they may be better fingered higher up the neck of the guitar, perhaps using the transposable shapes of the bar-chords. The positions of these may be found in most chord books. Shorter versions of the chords are often possible, for example, Eaug. and F♯m could be played as four-note chords rather than six. Similarly, a different fingering may sometimes be used for the same chord. The most suitable chord form will depend on the chord changes involved.

Michael Stimpson

Chords shown: A, A⁶, A⁷, A⁷sus⁴, Amaj⁷, A⁹, A⁹sus⁴, A⁹aug⁵, Am, Am♯⁶, Am⁷, Am/G, Aaug, Adim, B♭, B♭⁷, B, B⁷, B⁹, Bm, Bm⁷, Bdim, C, C⁷, Cmaj⁷, C⁹, C⁹sus⁴, C/D, Cm, C♯, C♯⁷

GUITAR CHORDS

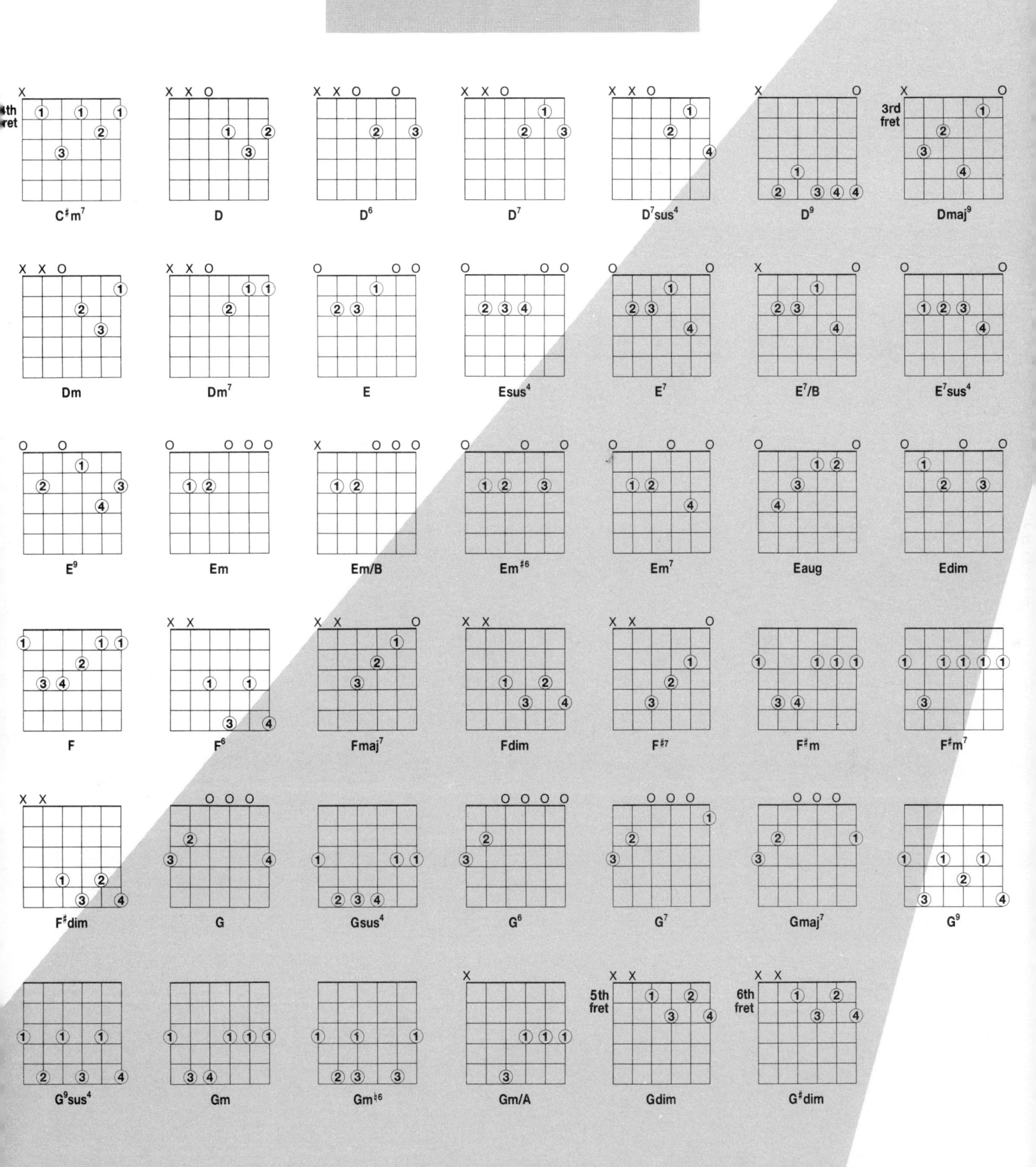

Printed by Halstan & Co. Ltd., Amersham, Bucks., England